I0428520

Datacenter Relocation Roadmap

How to Plan and Execute a Seamless Move

Csaba Szeles

Datacenter Relocation Roadmap

How to Plan and Execute a Seamless Move

Csaba Szeles

Contents

1 About this book

Embark on an extraordinary journey with "Datacenter Relocation Roadmap," an invaluable and comprehensive guide that will lead you to triumph in your datacenter relocation endeavor. Whether you find yourself at the beginning stages of contemplation or already knee-deep in the relocation process, congratulations on embarking on this transformative path. This book is here to accompany you every step of the way, providing expert guidance and insights to ensure your success.

Datacenter relocation goes beyond the physical transfer of equipment; it encompasses a complex array of factors, including organizational objectives, intricate IT infrastructure, and adept project management. Within the pages of this book, you will discover a treasure trove of knowledge that delves deep into each of these critical components.

By meticulously exploring the intricacies of datacenter relocation, my goal is to arm you with the necessary tools, strategies, and insights to navigate this complex undertaking with confidence. From feasibility assessments to informed decision-making, from addressing missing information to the pivotal day of movement, this comprehensive roadmap leaves no stone unturned.

Whether you are a seasoned professional seeking guidance or embarking on your very first datacenter relocation, this book is your trusted companion throughout the journey. Together, let us embark on a path that leads to a successful and stress-free datacenter relocation, ensuring the continuity of your organization's technological prowess and establishing a solid foundation for a prosperous future.

Migrating a datacenter is a complex process that demands meticulous planning, coordination, and execution for a seamless transition. Whether you are relocating to a new location, consolidating datacenters, or upgrading your infrastructure, this book will serve as your step-by-step guide, ensuring a successful move.

It's important to note that this book serves as an illustration, showcasing examples using specific technologies such as iSeries or TSM backup systems. However, if you are utilizing different vendors or solutions, feel free to substitute them accordingly. The primary purpose is to provide you with valuable reference points and insights as you navigate your datacenter relocation journey.

Throughout the following chapters, you will come across task lists that serve as valuable tool to aid you in your datacenter relocation journey. These resources are designed to provide structure and clarity, allowing you to track progress and make necessary adjustments along the way.

It's important to note that these tasks are not set in stone and can be modified to suit your specific requirements. They offer flexibility, allowing you to prioritize and rearrange them based on your unique circumstances and project timeline.

Remember, the key is to adapt and modify these tasks to best suit your datacenter relocation project. By doing so, you can ensure a smooth and efficient process, minimizing risks and maximizing success. Embrace the flexibility and leverage these resources to create a roadmap that works best for you.

1.1 Marketing Over Matter

My biggest problem with shiny pamphlets is that they are often marketed as informative and useful resources, yet they lack any real substance. Instead of providing practical information and tips, they're often filled with buzzwords and vague concepts that don't actually help the reader.

As someone who is interested in learning about various topics and applying that knowledge to real-life situations, I find it frustrating that so many resources are more concerned with looking impressive than actually providing value. This is especially true for books that claim to offer insight on complex subjects. Without clear and concise information, these books can be more confusing than helpful.

This book covers a range of topics related to datacenter relocation, including the following:

- The importance of thorough planning and project management in datacenter relocation.
- Considerations for selecting the right datacenter tier rating for specific business needs.
- The significance of financial calculations and value assessment in the decision-making process of datacenter relocation.
- Strategies for gathering missing information and ensuring comprehensive understanding of the relocation project.
- Best practices for creating a comfortable and functional workspace within the datacenter environment.

Whether you're a CIO, IT manager, or a datacenter professional, this book is designed to provide you with the knowledge and tools needed to successfully relocate your datacenter. I understand that relocating a datacenter is no small feat, and the process can be daunting even for the most experienced professionals. That's why I've created a comprehensive guide that covers everything from selecting the right location to managing the logistics of the move.

So, let's get started on your datacenter relocation journey!

2 To Move or Not to Move

Datacenter relocation is often driven by a multitude of external factors that can impact the efficiency, cost-effectiveness, and overall success of an organization. As an IT professional, it is crucial to consider and assess these factors to provide valuable insights and guidance throughout the decision-making process.

2.1 Factors Influencing Datacenter Relocation

Cost Considerations: One of the primary external factors that can trigger a datacenter move is cost. Fluctuating expenses such as electricity, real estate, or datacenter space can significantly impact an organization's bottom line. By analyzing the potential cost savings or increased efficiency that a relocation may offer, IT professionals can provide valuable input to management and facilitate informed decision-making.

Regulatory and Compliance Requirements: Government regulations and industry standards are dynamic forces that can drive the need for a datacenter relocation. Changes in security, privacy, or data protection regulations may necessitate a move to ensure compliance and mitigate legal risks. IT professionals play a critical role in assessing the impact of these regulations and guiding organizations towards meeting the required standards through strategic relocation.

Strategic Alignment and Market Access: Changes in business strategies, leadership, or market dynamics can also act as external triggers for datacenter relocation. A company may seek to relocate its datacenter to align with new strategic objectives, be closer to its customer base, or gain access to emerging markets. IT professionals can evaluate the potential benefits and risks associated with such moves, enabling organizations to adapt and thrive in evolving business landscapes.

Scalability and Future Growth: As businesses evolve and expand, Your datacenter needs may outgrow Your existing infrastructure. A datacenter relocation can provide an opportunity to consolidate multiple locations, centralize operations, and enhance scalability. IT professionals can assess the current and future requirements, ensuring that the chosen relocation strategy aligns with the organization's long-term growth plans.

Technological Advancements: Advancements in technology can render existing datacenter infrastructures obsolete or less efficient. The need to adopt emerging technologies, such as cloud computing or virtualization, may trigger a datacenter move to modernize and optimize IT operations. IT professionals can evaluate the feasibility and benefits of incorporating new technologies into the relocation process.

Understanding the various external factors that influence datacenter relocation is essential for making informed decisions and planning a successful migration. By considering factors such as cost, regulatory compliance, strategic alignment, scalability, and technological advancements.

2.2 Navigating the Decision-Making Process

IT clients have high expectations when it comes to availability, often aiming for the coveted "five nines" standard of 99.999%. However, achieving this level of availability requires more than just investing in robust computer hardware and software. It also necessitates a site infrastructure that can effectively support these ambitious goals. The site's overall tier rating is determined by various subsystem ratings, including power, cooling, and distribution.

With expertise in information technology, your role in the decision-making process is critical. You need to assess the technical feasibility of a move, identify potential risks, and provide recommendations on the best course of action. You may also need to consider factors such as network connectivity, disaster recovery, and compliance requirements when evaluating potential new locations for the datacenter.

Once the trigger for a datacenter relocation has been initiated, the architect assumes the crucial responsibility of presenting viable solutions and alternative options. As a skilled IT professional, your role naturally involves providing management with a range of choices to consider. However, the ultimate decision of whether to proceed with the move or not hinges on intricate financial calculations and the potential value that the relocation can yield.

Navigating the decision-making process can be a multifaceted endeavor, as it involves engaging with diverse stakeholders and factoring in various considerations.

2.3 Introduction to Feasibility Studies for DC Relocation

A feasibility study is a crucial step in any datacenter relocation project. It is a document that provides a detailed analysis of the project's feasibility, outlining the risks, benefits, costs, and potential problems associated with the move. As an IT professional, you may have written or read a feasibility study at some point in your career. The feasibility study is not a Low-Level Design (LLD) or a High-Level Design (HLD). Instead, it provides factual information about the project's feasibility.

Depending on the size of the infrastructure, a feasibility study can be as long as 20 to 80 pages. It is similar to writing a thesis in a university. However, it doesn't require you to be a Jedi or an expert in the matrix. You only need to have a good understanding of your area of expertise.

The primary aim of the feasibility study is to collect the company's needs, systematize them, and examine their feasibility by analyzing potential solutions. It also aims to identify the risks involved in the project's implementation and propose solutions to mitigate them.

To prepare a comprehensive feasibility study, You can use several methods to gather requirements, constraints, and information. These include consulting the project call for tender and terms of reference, personal interviews with the company's system admins, reviewing IT solution vendors' documentation, drawing on previous experience in designing and implementing similar systems, and even exchanging experiences with other Experienced Professionals or just simply read this book.

In conclusion, a feasibility study is a necessary tool for any IT professional involved in a datacenter relocation project. It provides a structured approach to assess the project's feasibility, risks, and benefits and helps identify potential solutions to mitigate risks. However, the question remains: Where does one begin?

2.4 Never trust the numbers the client tells you.

As an experienced professional, you've probably heard the phrase "never trust the numbers the client tells you" more times than you can count. That's because, in many cases, clients tend to overestimate their infrastructure's capacity or underestimate the costs of a datacenter move. That's why a thorough feasibility study is essential before embarking on any relocation project.

In my quest to provide a comprehensive guide, I have carefully assembled a thoughtfully curated collection of chapter titles that not only capture the essence of each topic but also offer an extended understanding of what should be included within.

Methodology for the feasibility study In this Chapter you have to discuss the methodology for conducting a feasibility study, including gathering information from stakeholders, conducting site surveys, and analyzing existing infrastructure. You will also explore different tools and techniques for data collection, such as interviews, surveys, and automated data collection.

The objectives and expected results It focuses on the objectives and expected results of the datacenter consolidation and relocation project. You'll discuss the benefits of consolidation, such as cost savings, improved efficiency, and reduced complexity. You'll also examine the challenges of consolidation and how to overcome them. Finally, You'll explore the expected outcomes of the relocation project, such as reduced downtime, increased performance, and improved disaster recovery capabilities.

Project Objectives It refers to the specific goals that the datacenter consolidation and relocation project aims to achieve. These objectives can vary depending on the needs of the organization, but they should always be clearly defined and communicated to all stakeholders.

Main objective of the Project The main objective of the project is to consolidate and relocate the datacenter while minimizing downtime and ensuring minimal impact to the business operations. The project aims to identify the optimal location for the new datacenter, develop a comprehensive plan for the migration process, and execute the plan with minimal disruptions. In addition, the project seeks to optimize the use of resources and reduce operational costs while ensuring that the new datacenter meets the business's current and future needs. To achieve these objectives, the project team will need to conduct a thorough feasibility study, assess the risks and challenges, and develop a detailed project plan that considers all aspects of the datacenter consolidation and relocation.

Project scope The project scope outlines the boundaries and limitations of the datacenter relocation project. It defines the goals, deliverables, tasks, timelines, and resources required for the project's successful completion. The scope of the project must be clearly defined and documented to ensure that all stakeholders have a common understanding of the project's objectives and expectations. It also helps to prevent scope creep, which can lead to project delays, increased costs, and lower quality outcomes. A well-defined project scope enables project managers to manage the project effectively, control risks, and ensure that the project stays on track towards meeting its goals.

Project boundaries Project boundaries refer to the limits or constraints that define the scope of the project. These boundaries can be physical, organizational, technical, or any other constraints that affect the project's feasibility and success.

For example, physical boundaries may include limitations on the size or location of the new datacenter, while organizational boundaries may include restrictions on the availability of human resources or budget. Technical boundaries may include compatibility issues between the existing and new datacenter infrastructure.

It is important to clearly define the project boundaries to ensure that the project objectives are achievable and realistic within the given constraints. This will help to avoid scope creep and ensure that the project is completed on time and within budget.

Project deadline and duration The project deadline and duration are critical factors that need to be determined during the feasibility study. It is important to have a clear understanding of the time frame within which the project needs to be completed. The project duration can vary depending on the complexity and scale of the datacenter relocation project. The feasibility study should include a detailed timeline that outlines all the tasks, milestones, and deliverables, along with their estimated durations.

(This chapter will need to be revisited and updated once the feasibility study is complete. As the project progresses, the initial timeline and deadlines may need to be adjusted to account for unforeseen obstacles or changes in requirements)

Additionally, the feasibility study should also factor in any external dependencies that could impact the project timeline. For instance, if the datacenter relocation involves working with external vendors or service providers, their availability and timelines should be considered as well.

(Consider the example of an internet service provider. When moving to a new data center, it is important to assess whether the ISP is available in the new location and if they have a physical connection (L1). Additionally, if public IPs are being used, it is necessary to determine if they are transferrable or not in case of the ISP is unavailable.)

It is also essential to consider the project deadline carefully. In some cases, the deadline might be non-negotiable due to business or regulatory requirements. In other cases, there may be some flexibility, but it is important to have a realistic and achievable deadline. The feasibility study should include a detailed analysis of the resources required to complete the project within the given timeline, including the availability of skilled personnel, equipment, and budget. This analysis will help ensure that the project can be completed successfully within the allocated time frame.

Expected impact of project implementation Through the implementation of the Data Center Consolidation and Relocation project, the company can achieve several benefits that meet their needs. These include the following:

- More efficient and redundant operations through automation and resource optimization.
- Ensuring scalability to support future growth.

- High-speed network connectivity to support the infrastructure.
- Compliance with operational security guidelines to ensure data protection and privacy.
- Adequate computing capacity to meet the company's requirements.
- Full geo-redundant deployment to ensure business continuity in the event of a disaster.
- Use of industry standard compliant components for consistency and compatibility.
- Elimination of all End-of-Support and End-of-Life assets, reducing the risk of failure and increasing reliability. It is essential to assess and understand the expected impact of the project implementation to ensure that the objectives are met, and the benefits are achieved.

As we draw closer to the conclusion of outlining the objectives and expected results, there is one final goal that must be addressed: Financial Goals

Financial Goals We need to define the following goals:

- Low maintenance costs: The new data center should have low maintenance costs to help the company save money and time in the long run. The project should aim to identify and eliminate any unnecessary costs related to maintenance.
- Cost-effective expandability: The company needs to ensure that the new data center is scalable and can accommodate future growth. The project should aim to provide a cost-effective solution for expanding the system without incurring high costs.
- Cost-effective scalability: The project should ensure that the data center is scalable in a cost-effective manner. This means that the system can be easily upgraded and expanded as the company grows without incurring high costs.

- Useful life of the system should be defined as (at least) 5 years: The project should aim to provide a system that is durable and can last for at least five years. This will help the company save costs associated with frequent replacements and upgrades.
- Aim to reuse existing vendor solutions already available to the operator, and to ensure integration and compatibility with existing systems: The project should aim to reuse existing vendor solutions to the extent possible. This will help the company save costs associated with purchasing new solutions. The project should also ensure that the new system is compatible with existing systems to avoid any disruptions to operations.

By meeting these objectives, the company can ensure a successful implementation of the DataCenter Consolidation and Relocation project while minimizing costs and maximizing efficiency.

Proposals for consolidation solutions Consolidating data centers can be a complex task, and there are various factors to consider before deciding on the right solution. Proposed Consolidation Solutions and Areas for Assessment (if applies) for example:

- iSeries
- pSeries
- x86
- VMware (virtualization layer)
- TSM (backup solutions)
- Storage
- NAS
- Voice network
- DataCenter Network (LAN+SAN)
- DMZ
- Temporary devices

The next step in the feasibility study is to analyze the areas identified for consolidation, taking into account several criteria. These criteria include:

- Sizing guidelines and information: This includes evaluating the size and capacity requirements for each area identified for consolidation, and determining whether they can be met with the proposed solutions.
- Current redundancy and fault-tolerant operation: This involves assessing the existing redundancy and fault-tolerant capabilities of each area, and identifying any gaps that need to be addressed.
- Recommended design: Based on the sizing guidelines and other requirements, a recommended design should be proposed for each area to ensure optimal performance and efficiency.
- Manufacturer support: The feasibility study should consider whether the proposed solutions are supported by the manufacturers and vendors of the hardware and software. To further elaborate, it is crucial to note that the devices currently in use are approaching or have already reached End-of-Support and End-of-Life status. This poses a significant risk to the overall system's stability and security, as these devices will no longer receive manufacturer support, including firmware updates and patches. As a result, the consolidation project must prioritize the replacement of these devices with more up-to-date and supported alternatives to ensure the system's longevity and resilience.
- Location and physical parameters: This involves assessing the physical space, power, cooling, and environmental requirements for each area, and determining whether the proposed solutions can be accommodated.
- Datacenter placement: To determine the optimal placement of datacenter equipment, several factors must be analyzed from multiple perspectives. These include:

- Size of the asset to be purchased, measured in units
- The device's dimensions, including width, depth, and height
- The weight of the device
- Cooling requirements, including the direction of cooling airflow
- The power required by the device, measured in watts
- Power requirements, including voltage (230V) and power connector type
- The presence of redundant power supplies
- Heat load, measured in BTUs per hour
- The quantity of devices to be supplied
- Model and serial numbers of the devices

Analyzing these factors will enable us to determine the best placement for the equipment and ensure that all devices are supported and function optimally.

- Network requirement (FC - Ethernet): The study should consider the network requirements for each area, including the need for Fibre Channel (FC) or Ethernet connectivity (how many ETH/FC Interface is required)
- Storage requirements: Finally, the study should assess the storage requirements for each area, and determine whether the proposed solutions can meet these requirements.

Summary This chapter is of critical importance to C-level managers as it outlines the key objectives and expected results of the DataCenter Consolidation and Relocation project. The main objective of the project is to consolidate the company's devices into a single, more efficient phase or improving the current level of service.

In addition, the chapter discusses the scope and boundaries of the project, as well as the deadline and expected duration of the implementation. It also highlights the potential impact of the project on the company, including highly automated redundant operations, efficient resource utilization, compliance with operational security guidelines, and the elimination of all End-of-Support, End-of-Life assets.

Furthermore, the chapter proposes various consolidation solutions and areas that need to be assessed, such as iSeries, pSeries, x86, VMware, TSM, Storage, NAS, Voice network, DataCenter Network, DMZ, and Temporary devices. It also emphasizes the importance of analyzing these areas based on sizing guidelines and information, current redundancy and fault-tolerant operation, recommended design, manufacturer support, location and physical parameters, datacenter placement, network requirements, and storage requirements.

Overall, this chapter provides a comprehensive overview of the project and its potential impact, making it a crucial read for C-level managers who will be responsible for overseeing the implementation and ensuring its success.

3 The Importance of Quantitative Analysis

To ensure the success of the project, it's essential to have a clear understanding of the feasibility study, including the numbers, figures, and timeline.

A combination of waterfall and agile methodology can be used to tackle any unforeseen issues that may arise during the project. In order to keep track of the project progress and ensure timely delivery, it's recommended to use a reliable project management tool. This will help the team to stay on track, prioritize tasks, and monitor deadlines, ultimately leading to the successful implementation of the project.

For my own project, I have developed a framework using a project management tool, as depicted in the image. Throughout this book, I will delve into each task and provide comprehensive explanations to guide you.

Project Skeleton

3.1 Charting Your Path to Success

The planning phase of the project is one of the most critical and time-consuming parts. It is common to face missing or inaccurate information during this phase, such as outdated or incomplete documentation, lack of proper asset database, missing rack drawings, and incomplete device inventory. To address these issues, it is crucial to allocate adequate time for assessments and data gathering.

It is also essential to determine which devices are at their end-of-support life, as they will need to be replaced or upgraded as part of the consolidation process. Additionally, factors such as rack capacity, power and cooling requirements, and telco connections must be considered to determine the most suitable location for the new data center.

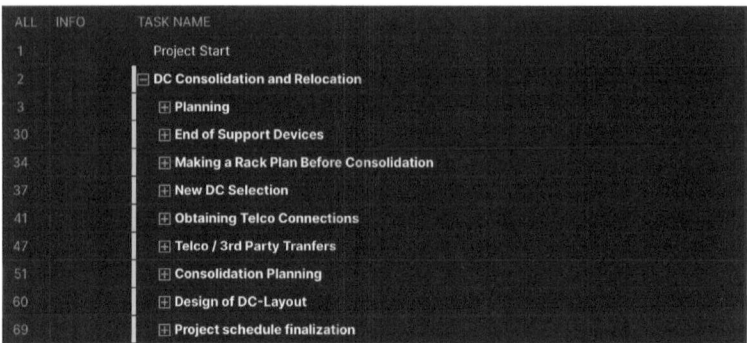

DC Consolidation and Relocation

If consolidation is part of the project plan, a clear strategy must be established to minimize the impact on the business operations. This may include Planning, phasing out outdated devices, migrating services and applications to new infrastructure, and decommissioning redundant equipment. Also the task include acquiring Telco connections, planning the consolidation strategy designing the layout of the new data center, and finalizing the schedule.

3.2 Collecting Missing Information

Acquiring missing information can be a challenging aspect of the project. As mentioned earlier, your role is not only to update the existing data but also to identify what is missing. To assist you in this process, I have compiled a list of tasks to help you start thinking about what you have and what you don't have. You may need to modify or expand on these tasks to suit your specific needs.

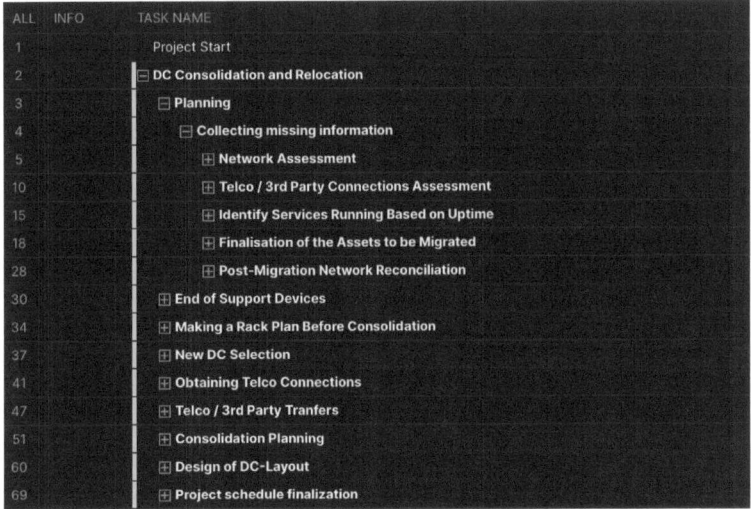

Collecting Missing Information

Some tasks to consider when collecting missing information include:

- Reviewing current documentation and identifying any gaps or inconsistencies
- Conducting interviews with key stakeholders to gather information and clarify details
- Conducting site visits to assess the current infrastructure and identify any issues

- Reviewing contracts and agreements with vendors and service providers to ensure all information is up to date and accurate

3.2.1 Network Assessment

As we move into the network assessment phase of the project, there are several key areas that need to be examined to ensure a successful consolidation and relocation effort. These include an analysis of the L1, L2, and L3 connections within the current data center infrastructure.

ALL	INFO	TASK NAME
1		Project Start
2		⊟ DC Consolidation and Relocation
3		⊟ Planning
4		⊟ Collecting missing information
5		⊟ Network Assessment
6		L1 Connections
7		L2 Connections
8		L3 Connections
9		Network Architecture Map

Network Assessment

When examining L1 connections, it is important to determine whether physical cables are in place or if new ones will need to be installed in the new DC. You'll also need to identify the location and capacity of network distribution devices such as switches and routers in case of free interface capacity.

For L2 connections, focus on understanding the current VLAN configurations, the availability of redundant paths, and the capacity of the core network devices. This can come handy when you move workload between 2 DC.

Finally, when analyzing L3 connections, it is essential to identify the current routing protocols, the security and access control mechanisms in place, and the overall network design.

As you work through these areas, document any missing information or discrepancies in the existing documentation. This information will be critical in ensuring that the new data center infrastructure is designed and implemented effectively.

Finally, it is important to note that once all the necessary information has been collected, it can be helpful to create a network architecture map. This map will provide a visual representation of the network and its components, allowing for easier identification of potential areas for improvement or optimization. The network architecture map can also be used as a reference tool for troubleshooting and maintenance tasks, ensuring that the network remains stable and efficient.

3.2.2 Telco/3rd party Connections Assessment

The Telco/3rd Party Connections Assessment is a crucial task that can significantly impact the relocation lead time. It is important to conduct a technical survey of the current internet service provider (ISP) to determine the speed and type of internet connection. Additionally, it is essential to review contracts and consider pricing and termination policies.

ALL	INFO	TASK NAME
1		Project Start
2		⊟ DC Consolidation and Relocation
3		⊟ Planning
4		⊟ Collecting missing information
5		⊞ Network Assessment
10		⊟ Telco / 3rd Party Connections Assessment
11		Technical Survey
12		Collecting Contact Information
13		Review of Contracts
14		Collection of Relocation Lead Times
15		⊞ Identify Services Running Based on Uptime
18		⊞ Finalisation of the Assets to be Migrated
28		⊞ Post-Migration Network Reconciliation

Telco Assessment

During this task, you will need to communicate with the account manager/salesperson and technical team of the ISP to ensure a smooth transition. Having on-call numbers for technical support can be helpful in case of any issues during the relocation process.

It is essential to determine the lead time required for the ISP to provide service at the new data center location. In some cases, the lead time may be longer than expected, and it can add at least 30 days to the project timeline. It is recommended to add this lead time to the project gantt chart to avoid any delays.

There may be situations where the original plan for a direct connection to a new data center location may not be feasible or practical due to cost, availability, or other factors. In such cases, it is important to explore alternative options and solutions to keep the project on track.

For instance, I have encountered a scenario in which we were unable to establish a direct connection to the new data center location due to limited availability and high installation costs. However, we were able to find a viable alternative by re-routing the connection through a third data center that had a 1Gbit/s direct connection to the new location. This allowed us to continue our operations without significant delays or additional costs.

It is important to consider all available options and evaluate them based on their feasibility, cost, and impact on the project timeline. Flexibility and creativity are often key to finding alternative solutions that can keep the project moving forward.

3.2.3 Identify services running based on uptime

To ensure uninterrupted service during the relocation process, it is important to identify which services need to be running 24/7. This includes critical services such as webshops, production databases, and call centers. Once these services have been identified, it is important to estimate the potential outage time in terms of Recovery Time Objective (RTO) and Recovery Point Objective (RPO).

RTO refers to the maximum amount of time a system can be down without causing significant harm to the business, while RPO refers to the maximum amount of data loss that can be tolerated. By estimating the RTO and RPO for each service, you can develop a plan to minimize downtime and data loss during the relocation process.

ALL	INFO	TASK NAME
1		Project Start
2		⊟ DC Consolidation and Relocation
3		⊟ Planning
4		⊟ Collecting missing information
5		⊞ Network Assessment
10		⊞ Telco / 3rd Party Connections Assessment
15		⊟ Identify Services Running Based on Uptime
16		Databases
17		Other SaaS Services
18		⊞ Finalisation of the Assets to be Migrated
28		⊞ Post-Migration Network Reconciliation

Identify Services

In addition, it is important to document any dependencies between services to ensure that they can be moved together without causing disruptions. This may involve coordinating with different teams or vendors to ensure that all necessary components are moved in a coordinated manner.

Overall, careful planning and coordination is essential to ensure that critical services remain operational during the relocation process and that downtime and data loss are minimized.

In order to minimize downtime during the move, it may be helpful to add additional devices to the environment. One way to achieve this is by using a Layer 2 extended VLAN to create a duplicate network environment at the new location. This can allow for the high-availability or active-passive systems to be moved to the new location with minimal downtime or impact. It is important to ensure that the necessary hardware and software are in place to support this type of network architecture, and that any potential issues or compatibility concerns are addressed prior to the move. By implementing this strategy, you can reduce the risk of disruption and ensure a smooth transition to the new location.

3.2.4 Finalisation of the assets to be migrated

Finalizing the list of assets to be migrated is a critical step in the relocation process. Based on my experience, it's common for third-party providers to replace their old network devices before the move. This ensures that their old devices won't cause any problems during the migration, and they can easily reroute traffic once the move is in progress. It's also a good idea to have a private check to verify the connectivity of the new devices. This can be achieved by providing a test public IP in their network devices or by putting a Mikrotik at the end of the cable and pinging that device.

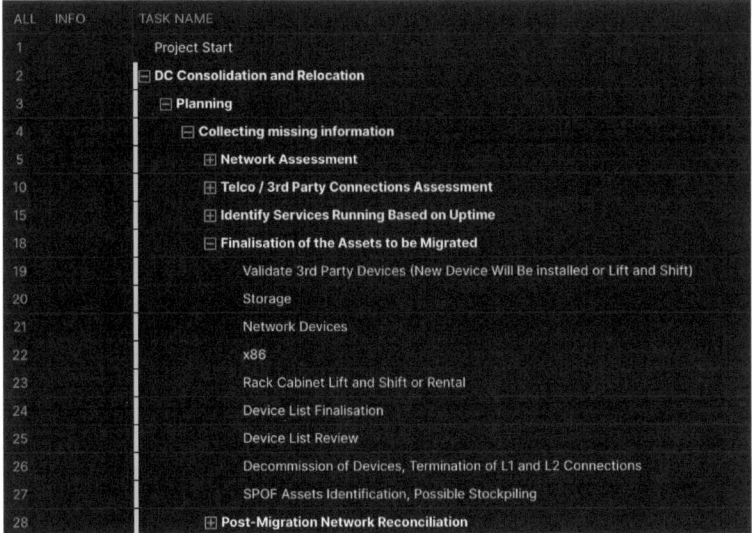

ALL	INFO	TASK NAME
1		Project Start
2		⊟ DC Consolidation and Relocation
3		⊟ Planning
4		⊟ Collecting missing information
5		⊞ Network Assessment
10		⊞ Telco / 3rd Party Connections Assessment
15		⊞ Identify Services Running Based on Uptime
18		⊟ Finalisation of the Assets to be Migrated
19		Validate 3rd Party Devices (New Device Will Be installed or Lift and Shift)
20		Storage
21		Network Devices
22		x86
23		Rack Cabinet Lift and Shift or Rental
24		Device List Finalisation
25		Device List Review
26		Decommission of Devices, Termination of L1 and L2 Connections
27		SPOF Assets Identification, Possible Stockpiling
28		⊞ Post-Migration Network Reconciliation

Finalisation of the assets

Storage is another important consideration. When relocating, it's best to migrate to a new hybrid storage system to refresh your devices. This way, you can do an online migration between the two data centers using tools like VMware vSphere Replication. However, it's essential to have an offline backup of your data in case anything goes wrong during the migration. It can be daunting to move storages with the disks, but with proper planning and precautions, it can be done safely.

It's also essential to consider the type of replication you will use. In the case of IP, you won't have the option of FC replication. Instead, you will need to use replication tools like VMware vSphere Replication. On the other hand, if you have any tiype of WDM network, you can use FC replication to replicate your storage.

When it comes to moving data centers, it is always wise to evaluate your current infrastructure and determine what needs to be replaced or upgraded. If you have the opportunity, it is best to purchase new devices to ensure that they are up to date and have the latest features. If purchasing new devices is not an option, consider renting equipment during the move to ensure that you have the necessary hardware.

In terms of x86 servers, if you are using virtualization, it is likely that your servers are already oversized, and you can migrate some of the "unused" servers to the new location. This can help reduce costs and ensure that you have enough resources to support your operations.

Another critical aspect of a data center move is the rack cabinet question. Will you buy or rent? It is possible to create an RFI (Request for Information) for the new data center selection, where you can include an optional item for rack cabinet renting. If you have a lot of unused or barely used rack cabinets, it is useful to use them and ensure that you have enough PDU (Power Distribution Units) with the correct number of C13 and C19 connection outlets. If you are not purchasing new PDUs, make sure to note the brand in the DC selection RFI to ensure compatibility.

After completing the device list finalization, it is important to review the list and remove any unused devices from the IT infrastructure. However, it is crucial to keep a grace period of at least 1-2 weeks before actually disconnecting and removing them from the environment.

During the assessment, you may have identified some single points of failure (SPOF) devices. It is important to decide whether to purchase additional devices to remedy those problems or start stockpiling to have backup devices available. Keep in mind that some devices may have been running for years and may not start up after being unplugged and moved to a new location. Therefore, having a backup plan in place is important, as a next business day solution may not be feasible, especially if the move takes place on a Friday night, as the next business day would be Monday or Tuesday.

Additionally, it is important to conduct thorough testing and validation of all devices and services before and after the move. This includes checking the connectivity and functionality of all devices, applications, and services, and ensuring that all backups and disaster recovery plans are in place and tested. It is also recommended to have a fallback plan in case any issues arise during the move, such as having spare equipment on hand or alternative connectivity options.

3.2.5 Post-migration network reconciliation

After the assessment process, it is crucial to conduct a post-migration network reconciliation. This reconciliation process involves verifying that all network devices are configured properly, including switches, routers, firewalls, load balancers, and any other network appliances.

Post-migration

In addition, it is important to verify that all IP addresses, VLANs, and routing protocols are properly configured and updated. Any issues or discrepancies found during the reconciliation process should be addressed promptly to ensure that the network is operating efficiently and effectively.

Furthermore, it is recommended to perform load testing and latency testing to ensure that the network is performing at an optimal level.

This will help identify any bottlenecks or areas where network performance can be improved.

Finally, it is important to update all relevant network documentation to reflect the changes made during the assessment process. This includes updating network diagrams, IP address lists, and any other relevant documentation to ensure that the network is properly documented for future reference.

3.3 Essential Steps for a Seamless Transition

After collecting all the necessary information about the network and migrating devices, it's time to dive into other important topics that can make or break a successful data center migration. In this chapter, we will explore the key considerations that need to be made when planning a data center migration.

3.3.1 End of Support devices

ALL	INFO	TASK NAME
1		Project Start
2		⊟ DC Consolidation and Relocation
3		⊞ Planning
30		⊟ End of Support Devices
31		Device List Assessment
32		Device List Review
33		Decision on EoS Devices (Possible SPoF)

End of Support

When it comes to dealing with end-of-support (EOS) devices, it is important to have a clear plan in place. These devices are no longer receiving security updates or patches, which can make them vulnerable to cyber attacks.

The first step in dealing with EOS devices is to conduct a device list assessment. This involves identifying all devices that are no longer supported and determining which ones are critical to the business. Once this assessment is complete, it is important to conduct a device list review to ensure that no devices have been missed.

Once you have a complete list of EOS devices, you will need to make a decision on what to do with them. If the device is not a single point of failure (SPOF) and is not critical to the business, it may be acceptable to continue using it until it fails. However, if the device is a SPOF or critical to the business, it is important to take action.

One option is to replace the EOS device with a new one. However, sometimes replacing an old device can be more complicated than expected. For example, an old device may be running on outdated software or hardware that is no longer supported by newer devices. This can lead to compatibility issues and unexpected downtime.

In some cases, it may be more practical to stockpile replacement parts for EOS devices instead of immediately replacing them. This can buy some time while a longer-term replacement plan is put in place. However, it is important to keep in mind that stockpiling replacement parts is not a long-term solution and eventually, the device will need to be replaced.

In any case, it is important to have a plan in place for dealing with EOS devices. Neglecting to address these devices can lead to security vulnerabilities, unexpected downtime, and even financial losses for the business.

3.3.2 Making a rack plan before consolidation

ALL	INFO	TASK NAME
1		Project Start
2		⊟ DC Consolidation and Relocation
3		⊞ Planning
30		⊞ End of Support Devices
34		⊟ Making a Rack Plan Before Consolidation
35		*Network Survey Completed*
36		*The Device List to be Migrated can be Considered Final*

Making a Rack Plan

Before moving forward with the consolidation process, it's important to make a rack plan. The rack plan helps to organize and manage the physical equipment that will be moved to the new data center. This includes devices such as servers, storage, and network equipment.

A network survey should have already been completed to gather information on the devices that will be migrated. This information should include details such as the device name, model number, location, power consumption, and network connectivity requirements.

With the device list finalized, the rack plan can be created based on the physical dimensions and power requirements of each device. It's important to ensure that each device is placed in the appropriate location within the rack to optimize cooling and airflow.

Another consideration is the power distribution units (PDUs) that will be used to provide power to the equipment. The number and type of PDUs needed will depend on the number of devices and their power requirements. It's important to ensure that each PDU has the correct number and type of outlets to accommodate all of the devices in the rack.

By making a rack plan before consolidation, you can ensure that the equipment is organized and efficiently placed within the racks.

This will help to optimize cooling and airflow, reduce downtime during the move, and minimize the risk of damage to the equipment.

3.3.3 New DC selection

ALL	INFO	TASK NAME
1		Project Start
2		⊟ DC Consolidation and Relocation
3		⊞ Planning
30		⊞ End of Support Devices
34		⊞ Making a Rack Plan Before Consolidation
37		⊟ New DC Selection
38		RFP
39		Choose a Winner
40		Contract

New DC Selection

The first step in this process is to create a Request for Information (RFI) document. This document should include your device list, rack plan, and any other relevant information about your current infrastructure. The purpose of the RFI is to gather information from potential data center providers about their capabilities, pricing, and availability.

In the RFI I would go like this:

As part of the current RFI, we would like to assess the available solution models in case of relocating our data center to a new location.

The supplier's system/solution must partially or completely comply with the following professional functions and requirements:

Key criteria:

- Required area: 20 m2 (may decrease to ~15m2 during the process)

- Number of racks to be placed: 6 (may decrease to 4-5 during the process)
- Total power of devices: MAX 35,000 Watts
- Heat generation: MAX 100,000 BTU/h
- Lockable, separate cage/room (if possible, magnetic card access)
- Electrical energy (2 independent power supplies to the building)
- Within the server room - A+B independent power supply rail for the rack series.
- Redundant air conditioning, power supply, uninterruptible power supply (control and battery packs) + monitoring system
- Required humidity regulators, air filters.
- Our machine room temperature requirement: 22 Co +/- 2 Co
- Availability of some kind of power generator unit (e.g. diesel generator)
- Fire detection and firefighting system
- Possibility of independent track entry for data lines (provider lines)
- 24/7 physical protection, access control, and surveillance

Other requirements:

- We would like to use the data center as a service, which means that the service provider should provide all services related to the data center: cooling, heating, power supply (including physical security, access control, and surveillance).

In addition, please provide:

- Availability of the entire data center and other parameters, what they can provide, when planned maintenance is scheduled, what kind of outage and impact it will have.

- The load-bearing capacity of the raised floor in ton/m2
- Uninterruptible Power Supply (UPS) and generator capacity (how long they can provide power)
- Fire alarm and firefighting system (what extinguishing agents are used, where are they located - machine room, above the false ceiling, under the raised floor? Is there any residual waste/deposition from extinguishing agents?)
- Details on physical security (how does access control work, is there a metal detector, are the equipment to be brought in and out checked, logs, how long are the camera images available, can the rented area be alarmed, etc.)

We request the bidder to indicate any relevant references that can be shared, if available!

Other information:

- We cannot accept data center placement outside the country.
- Please provide the price per rack cabinet in the offer. We request a rental price for 6 standard (64x107x202) racks.
- Cold aisle containment is acceptable.
- Regarding the magnetic card and its type, we only have one expectation: it should be personalized, if possible with a photo. We would need a maximum of 10 cards + guest cards.
- Contract duration: 3+2 years (with the possibility of reducing the area during the contract period)
- How is equipment transportation in and out ensured? Including the transportation of components/equipment through the personnel gate.
- Also, the possibility of delivering equipment to the data center (including large-sized and heavy machines)

It is important to remember that selecting a new data center is not just about finding the cheapest option. You need to consider factors such as location, connectivity, security, and scalability. You also need to consider the reputation and track record of the data center provider.

Once you have received responses to your RFI, you can begin evaluating the options and narrowing down your choices. You may want to schedule site visits to potential data centers to see their facilities in person and meet with their staff.

Ultimately, the goal of selecting a new data center is to find a facility that can meet your current needs and support your future growth. By taking the time to carefully evaluate your options and make an informed decision, you can ensure a successful data center migration project.

3.3.4 Obtaining Telco connections

ALL	INFO	TASK NAME
1		Project Start
2		⊟ DC Consolidation and Relocation
3		⊞ Planning
30		⊞ End of Support Devices
34		⊞ Making a Rack Plan Before Consolidation
37		⊞ New DC Selection
41		⊟ Obtaining Telco Connections
42		Technical Definition of Telco Requirements
43		DC is Known
44		Telco RFP Run
45		Telco Selection (If Switching is Necessary)
46		Telco Contracting

Obraining Telco Connections

In order to secure new Telco connections for the data center, it is crucial to have a clear technical definition of what Telco services are required. This ensures that the appropriate service provider can be identified and selected. Once the Telco requirements are defined, the next step is to initiate a Request for Proposal (RFP) process to solicit offers from potential Telco providers.

During the RFP process, you will receive proposals from various

Telco providers. Based on the proposals, the Telco selection process can begin. In some cases, switching providers may be necessary, which can be a complicated and problematic process. For instance, changing the Telco provider may result in the need to reconfigure all public IPs, VPN connections, and other network settings. Therefore, it is advisable to carefully evaluate the pros and cons of switching providers, especially for large companies with multiple locations.

Once a Telco provider is selected, the contracting process can begin. This involves establishing the terms and conditions of the Telco services, including service level agreements (SLAs), pricing, and other important details. It is important to have a well-drafted contract to ensure that both parties fully understand their rights and responsibilities.

3.3.5 Telco / 3rd party transfers

ALL	INFO	TASK NAME
1		Project Start
2		⊟ DC Consolidation and Relocation
3		⊞ Planning
30		⊞ End of Support Devices
34		⊞ Making a Rack Plan Before Consolidation
37		⊞ New DC Selection
41		⊞ Obtaining Telco Connections
47		⊟ Telco / 3rd Party Tranfers
48		Sending Out Telco / 3rd Party Information Requests
49		Telco / 3rd Party Responses
50		Telco / 3rd Party Negotiations
51		⊞ Consolidation Planning
60		⊞ Design of DC-Layout
69		⊞ Project schedule finalization

Telco / 3rd Party

The process of transferring Telco or third-party services can be straightforward but requires careful management to ensure a smooth transition. Initially, information requests should be sent out to the relevant Telco or third-party service providers to gather data on the services they offer, including price of the transfer, terms and conditions, and technical specifications.

Drawing from my previous experience, I have found that depending on the new location, there may be a one-time migration fee charged. This could actually be important in cases where cost is a major consideration.

I believe that the service provider will likely perform the migration job effectively. However, it's important to note that the migration process requires adequate preparation, even though the actual switch may only take a few seconds. It's crucial to communicate any changes in your planned movement day to the service provider to avoid any complications.

If you have an L2 connection established between the two data centers, you have more flexibility with regards to when you can perform the switch. This can be a significant advantage in case there are any unforeseen circumstances that could delay the move. Therefore, it's recommended to consider establishing an L2 connection between the data centers to provide more flexibility in your migration planning.

3.3.6 Consolidation Planning

ALL	INFO	TASK NAME
1		Project Start
2		⊟ DC Consolidation and Relocation
3		⊞ Planning
30		⊞ End of Support Devices
34		⊞ Making a Rack Plan Before Consolidation
37		⊞ New DC Selection
41		⊞ Obtaining Telco Connections
47		⊞ Telco / 3rd Party Tranfers
51		⊟ Consolidation Planning
52		*Device List known*
53		⊟ Pre-migration consolidation agreement
54		⊟ Preparation of a technical description / plan of the tasks to be performed
55		Network Consolidation
56		Storage Consolidation
57		x86 Consolidation
58		Power Consolidation
59		Tape Library Consolidation
60		⊞ Design of DC-Layout
69		⊞ Project schedule finalization

Consolidation Planning

Consolidation planning is the next step in streamlining operations and reducing costs in an organization. To begin with, the device list needs to be finalized to identify the assets that need to be consolidated. Once this is done, a pre-migration consolidation agreement can be drafted to ensure all stakeholders are on board with the plan.

The next step is to prepare a technical description or plan detailing the tasks to be performed during the consolidation process. This plan should cover all aspects of consolidation, including network consolidation, storage consolidation, x86 consolidation, power consolidation, and tape library consolidation.

Network consolidation involves merging disparate networks into a single network infrastructure, resulting in improved efficiency and reduced maintenance costs. Storage consolidation involves pooling storage resources to make them more easily accessible and manageable. x86 consolidation involves reducing the number of physical servers through virtualization, which leads to cost savings and better resource utilization.

Power consolidation aims to optimize power usage by reducing the number of devices, power supplies, and cooling systems needed. This is achieved through techniques such as virtualization, consolidation of workloads, and adoption of energy-efficient hardware. Finally, tape library consolidation involves the migration of data from multiple tape libraries into a single consolidated tape library, resulting in improved backup and disaster recovery capabilities.

Overall, consolidation planning is a critical exercise that requires careful planning and execution to achieve its desired benefits.

3.3.7 Design of DC-Layout

ALL	INFO	TASK NAME
1		Project Start
2		⊟ DC Consolidation and Relocation
3		⊞ Planning
30		⊞ End of Support Devices
34		⊞ Making a Rack Plan Before Consolidation
37		⊞ New DC Selection
41		⊞ Obtaining Telco Connections
47		⊞ Telco / 3rd Party Tranfers
51		⊞ Consolidation Planning
60		⊟ Design of DC-Layout
61		DC known
62		Device list known
63		Telco, 3rd party known
64		Consolidation plan known
65		Device connection list known (L1)
66		Preparation of floor plan and rack allocation
67		Rack-Rack cabling design
68		Technical description for rack-rack cabling (If necessary)
69		⊞ Project schedule finalization

Design of DC-Layout

Once the rack layout has been almost finalized and all necessary information has been gathered, it is time to prepare a floorplan based on the RFI responses from the DC locations. In some cases, co-location spaces may have non-standard layouts, which requires careful planning and labeling of rack cabinets to ensure proper placement. Rack naming is particularly important for easy identification and management.

Another critical consideration is the rack-to-rack cabling. To minimize cabling, it is essential to select devices that can be cabled inside the rack cabinet as much as possible. This can be achieved through top-of-the-rack or end-of-row designs, depending on the number of rack cabinets involved. While the data center may offer their own solutions for rack-to-rack cabling, it is important to inquire about this service and any associated costs. If the data center does not provide any cables, an RFP may need to be drafted to procure the necessary materials.

Finally, this is an excellent opportunity to invest in a new cabling manager software to streamline the cabling process and facilitate ongoing management. This software can help ensure that all cables are properly labeled and tracked, reducing the risk of errors and facilitating future changes and upgrades. Overall, careful planning and attention to detail during the rack layout and cabling process can help ensure a smooth and efficient data center deployment.

3.3.8 Project schedule finalization

ALL	INFO	TASK NAME
1		Project Start
2		⊟ DC Consolidation and Relocation
3		⊞ Planning
30		⊞ End of Support Devices
34		⊞ Making a Rack Plan Before Consolidation
37		⊞ New DC Selection
41		⊞ Obtaining Telco Connections
47		⊞ Telco / 3rd Party Tranfers
51		⊞ Consolidation Planning
60		⊞ Design of DC-Layout
69		⊟ Project schedule finalization
70		*DC-DC Telco data connection establishment time is known*
71		*The establishment time of Telco / 3rd party transfers is known*
72		*Consolidation is known*
73		Create / update project schedule
74		Validation of project schedule, selection of moving date
75		Move-in date (planned) selected
76		Project schedule ready

Project Schedule Finalization

To ensure the smooth execution of the project, it is essential to create and update often a project schedule that outlines the tasks and timelines involved in the move. This schedule should be validated to ensure its accuracy, and a moving date should be selected based on the availability of resources and other factors.

Once the move-in date is chosen, the project schedule should be finalized and made available to all relevant parties.

It is important to keep in mind that unexpected events may occur, causing delays or changes to the project schedule. Therefore, it is recommended to build in some flexibility in the schedule and have contingency plans in place to address unforeseen issues. Regular monitoring and communication with all stakeholders can help ensure that the project stays on track and any potential issues are addressed promptly.

4 Planning for Success

Procurement in IT projects can be a challenging endeavor as it requires significant time and effort to navigate through their meticulous processes.

Working with procurement teams during the initial phase of a project can be particularly demanding as they typically require detailed information before proceeding. However, despite the challenges, it is crucial to work closely with them and provide all the necessary information.

The procurement phase is a critical stage where communication and transparency play a vital role in ensuring a smooth progression of the project. IT procurement teams often have strict protocols and procedures that must be followed, making it essential to collaborate effectively and align expectations.

Their attention to detail and adherence to policies help mitigate risks and ensure compliance with regulatory requirements. Effective communication during this phase is essential to establish clear timelines, address any potential challenges, and ensure a successful outcome.

4.1 Procurement

Welcome to the chapter on procurement, an essential aspect of the data center migration project. Procurement involves negotiating with the procurement team to acquire the necessary resources and services while adhering to budget constraints. In this chapter, we will discuss critical procurement considerations such as selecting appropriate racks, cables, and lift and shift services.

However, procurement is not just about acquiring resources; it also involves planning for potential risks and contingencies. This includes obtaining insurance coverage for equipment and infrastructure, identifying and addressing any single points of failure (SPOF) in the IT environment, and planning for end-of-support (EOS) devices. Third-party devices and special installation requirements also require additional attention and support.

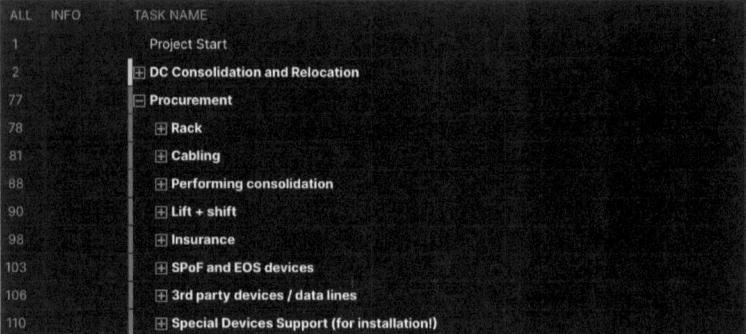

Procurement

Collaboration with the procurement team is crucial to ensure success. Effective communication and planning can help avoid delays, reduce costs, and ensure a seamless transition to the new data center. This chapter will provide insights into navigating the procurement process, identifying cost-effective solutions, and keeping the project objectives in mind.

4.1.1 Rack

ALL	INFO	TASK NAME
1		Project Start
2		⊞ DC Consolidation and Relocation
77		⊟ Procurement
78		⊟ Rack
79		Technical description of the racks required
80		Purchase or Rent

Rack

When it comes to rack procurement, there are several factors to consider. One of the first things to evaluate is whether you have enough spare rack cabinets available in your data center. This will depend on how much time you have to perform consolidation and whether the devices being decommissioned can be removed from their current cabinets. It's important to carefully inspect the cabling in front of the device to ensure that it won't cause any issues when you remove the device. You'll also need to check if there's enough free space to move the cabinets in case of the device fixed by the sides.

Timing is another crucial consideration. Do you have sufficient time and resources to perform the consolidation and decommission the devices? This can be a complex process that requires careful planning and coordination to minimize downtime and avoid potential risks.

If you don't have spare cabinets available, it may be easier to rent them from the data center owners. Many DCs offer 42-rack unit cabinets that are relatively affordable. Whether you decide to rent, purchase, or lift and shift the cabinets, it's essential to choose the right size and ensure that there is enough space for cabling and proper cable management. By considering these factors, you can make an informed decision about rack procurement and ensure a successful data center migration.

4.1.2 Cabling

ALL	INFO	TASK NAME
1		Project Start
2		⊞ DC Consolidation and Relocation
77		⊟ Procurement
78		⊞ Rack
81		⊟ Cabling
82		Technical description of the cabling required
83		Procurement for cabling (Will there be a patch rack or not?)
84		⊟ Purchase of new DC cables
85		Optics
86		RJ45
87		PDU + C13 and C19 cables

Cabling

One important consideration is determining the required number and length of cables for each device based on their interface usage. This includes not only RJ45 cables but also FC cables for storage devices. It's also important to note the cable type and connection type for any older devices that may require special cables.

Another important factor to consider is the type of cabling allowed by the data center. Some data centers may only allow CAT6 or CAT5EE cables, while others may require special cabling types. It's important to choose the right type of cable for a future-proof solution and not skimp on cost.

Choosing the color of the cables can also be helpful in managing cabling, such as using different colors for out-of-band management, in-band management, or backup. It's also a good idea to buy more cables than calculated, at least 20% more, to have spares on hand in case of unexpected needs.

It's also important to differentiate patch cables for patch cabinets and in-rack cabling cables. This will help to ensure that cables are properly managed and organized, and will make future maintenance and troubleshooting easier.

By carefully planning and executing cabling, the data center migration project can be completed smoothly and efficiently, ensuring minimal downtime and maximum performance.

4.1.3 Performing consolidation

ALL	INFO	TASK NAME
1		Project Start
2		⊞ DC Consolidation and Relocation
77		⊟ Procurement
78		⊞ Rack
81		⊞ Cabling
88		⊟ Performing consolidation
89		Technical specification clarification if needed
90		⊞ Lift + shift
98		⊞ Insurance
103		⊞ SPoF and EOS devices
106		⊞ 3rd party devices / data lines
110		⊞ Special Devices Support (for installation!)

Performing Consolidation

While performing the consolidation, it's important to keep in mind that unexpected issues may arise, so it's best to allocate extra time and resources for unforeseen problems. In addition, it's always beneficial to involve colleagues in the consolidation process as they may come up with innovative ideas to optimize the IT infrastructure.

During the consolidation process, it may be necessary to enlist the help of external companies or vendors to complete certain tasks. If IT infrastructure management is outsourced, it's crucial to have clear communication regarding pricing and to ensure that all tasks are completed within the agreed-upon timeframe.

To avoid delays and ensure a successful consolidation, it's important to maintain a comprehensive task list and to assign responsibilities to team members. Proper communication and documentation can help to identify and resolve any issues that arise during the consolidation process.

4.1.4 Lift + shift

ALL	INFO	TASK NAME
1		Project Start
2		⊞ DC Consolidation and Relocation
77		⊟ Procurement
78		⊞ Rack
81		⊞ Cabling
88		⊞ Performing consolidation
90		⊟ Lift + shift
91		DC known
92		Device list known
93		Consolidation is known
94		Technical description of the tasks required
95		RFP
96		RFP lead time
97		Contracting

Lift and Shift

While I have never had a bad experience with lift and shift, it can still be a daunting process. Thankfully, the team I have worked with in the past has always been professional and knowledgeable. That being said, there are some important points to consider when including lift and shift services in a request for proposal (RFP):

- We would like to draw the attention of the Bidder to the fact that certain equipment may exceed the normal load-bearing capacity of the raised floor. Therefore, the relocation of these equipment must be carried out with special attention and expertise. In the absence of this, the Bidder is fully responsible for any damage caused on site.

In addition, the Requestor will provide:

- an IT survey of the source server room
- planning and design of the destination server room
- preparation of equipment (e.g. data backup, proper shutdown and disconnection)

- manufacturer and service support
- reservation of replacement equipment and risk analysis
- moving plan and schedule preparation
- testing and communication planning
- power supply and cabling design of the destination server room
- installation, system start-up, and testing in the destination server room.

Detailed description of tasks related to IT equipment in the server room: The Requestor will hand over the server room equipment:

- labeled,
- properly shut down,
- disconnected (power supply, data cables),
- in rack-mounted condition.

The Bidder shall provide

- the necessary quantity and quality of packaging materials
- labor with appropriate expertise
- where available, the Requestor will provide the original packaging for certain equipment to the Bidder
- The Bidder shall arrange for the transportation of the equipment within the source site to the transport vehicle (truck, lorry), for which the Requestor shall provide assistance (appropriate transport corridor and loading space)
- The Bidder shall arrange for the transportation of the equipment to the destination server room address on an appropriate transport vehicle (truck, lorry), for which the Requestor shall provide assistance (appropriate unloading space)
- For the following equipment, the Bidder shall provide armed transportation and security: (If applies)

- The movement of the equipment within the destination server room building from the unloading point will be carried out by the DC experts
- If necessary, the Bidder shall arrange for the removal and further handling of the packaging materials.

Expectations of the Bidder

The Client has the following minimal expectations of the Bidder:

- Minimum of 2 owned box trucks with lift gates for main shipments
- Possibility to provide a 1.5t enclosed van for other shipments
- Possibility to provide a 0.6t pickup truck for other shipments
- Possibility to provide armed guards for transportation and loading/unloading
- At least 10 references of successful data center relocations involving IT equipment of 10 rack units or more
- At least 1 reference of successful relocation with armed guards
- Experience in handling complex, international IT equipment relocations is an advantage

The Client reserves the right to consider additional criteria provided by the Bidders.

This is just a hypothetical scenario, so feel free to adjust your expectations based on your individual needs and circumstances. It's important to identify what matters most to you and to communicate that clearly to others. By setting realistic and achievable expectations, you can help ensure that your needs are met and that everyone involved is on the same page.

4.1.5 Insurance

ALL	INFO	TASK NAME
1		Project Start
2		⊞ DC Consolidation and Relocation
77		⊟ Procurement
78		⊞ Rack
81		⊞ Cabling
88		⊞ Performing consolidation
90		⊞ Lift + shift
98		⊟ Insurance
99		*Device list known*
100		*Consolidation is known*
101		*Move-in date known*
102		RFP and RFP lead time
103		⊞ SPoF and EOS devices
106		⊞ 3rd party devices / data lines
110		⊞ Special Devices Support (for installation!)

Insurance

Insurance is an important aspect to consider in a Lift and Shift RFP. It's important to ask the delivery company if they have insurance and to review the conditions of their policy. Most of the lift and shift companies have insurance, but it's crucial to carefully review the terms of the policy. You should check if the policy covers the current value of your devices and what the insurance limits are.

It's also important to keep in mind that if you want to insure not just your devices, but also your data, it's going to be very expensive. There are only a limited number of insurance companies that are willing to insure your data, and the cost can be significant.

If you're considering insuring your data, be sure to research your options thoroughly and compare prices. It's also a good idea to consult with a professional to help you make an informed decision. Remember, protecting your data is important, but it's important to balance the cost with the level of risk you're willing to take.

4.1.6 SPoF and EOS devices

ALL	INFO	TASK NAME
1		Project Start
2		⊞ DC Consolidation and Relocation
77		⊟ Procurement
78		⊞ Rack
81		⊞ Cabling
88		⊞ Performing consolidation
90		⊞ Lift + shift
98		⊞ Insurance
103		⊟ SPoF and EOS devices
104		Run procurement for risky assets (Rental, extra support / insurance)
105		Testing of purchased equipment (If used)

SPoF and EOS

The following section pertains to SPoF (Single Point of Failure) and EOS (End of Support) devices. It is recommended to conduct a procurement process specifically for these risky assets, which may involve renting or acquiring extra support and insurance. In the case of purchasing used equipment, thorough testing should be conducted to ensure reliability. It is crucial to identify any SPoF or EOS devices in the system and take appropriate measures to mitigate the associated risks. Failure to do so may result in downtime, data loss, or other negative consequences.

I have personal knowledge of several companies that provide used devices or support for End of Support (EOS) and End of Life (EOL) devices. If your company is heavily reliant on these types of devices, it is highly recommended to consider procuring and negotiating with these types of companies. By doing so, you can potentially save a significant amount of money while still maintaining the necessary functionality of your equipment. However, it is important to carefully evaluate the reputation and quality of these companies, as well as any potential risks associated with using older equipment. Additionally, you should ensure that any agreements with these companies clearly outline their responsibilities for maintenance, repair, and support of the equipment.

4.1.7 3rd party devices / data lines

ALL	INFO	TASK NAME
1		Project Start
2		⊞ DC Consolidation and Relocation
77		⊟ Procurement
78		⊞ Rack
81		⊞ Cabling
88		⊞ Performing consolidation
90		⊞ Lift + shift
98		⊞ Insurance
103		⊞ SPoF and EOS devices
106		⊟ 3rd party devices / data lines
107		3rd party relocations preliminary info is available
108		Request for transfers (request for proposal)
109		Ordering transfers

3rd party

We have access to the parameters and contacts of the 3rd party telco lines. Therefore, the next step is to negotiate the procurement and transfers between these data lines.

To initiate the transfers, we need to make a request for proposal and order the transfers. If you decide to stick with the currently used telco lines, it is worth considering recontracting with them to obtain better prices or cheaper transfers. Always ask for the best and final offer to ensure that you are getting the best deal possible.

4.1.8 Special Devices Support (for installation!)

ALL	INFO	TASK NAME
1		Project Start
2		⊞ DC Consolidation and Relocation
77		⊟ Procurement
78		⊞ Rack
81		⊞ Cabling
88		⊞ Performing consolidation
90		⊞ Lift + shift
98		⊞ Insurance
103		⊞ SPoF and EOS devices
106		⊞ 3rd party devices / data lines
110		⊟ Special Devices Support (for installation!)
111		Tape Library
112		Power
113		Storage

Special Devices Support

Relocating devices is not a simple task, especially if they are covered by a live support contract. Attempting to move these devices without proper support may result in a loss of warranty or support coverage in the future.

Therefore, it is essential to discuss all aspects of the relocation with the vendor support team. This includes potential impacts on warranty or support coverage, the need for special tools, and the new maintenance location. Planning ahead and seeking advice from the vendor support team can help prevent any issues during and after the relocation process.

4.1.9 New DC Layout

ALL	INFO	TASK NAME
1		Project Start
2		⊞ DC Consolidation and Relocation
77		⊞ Procurement
114		⊟ New DC Layout
115		New DC selected
116		New DC environment Layout prep (Grid, Electricity, etc.)
117		Exact internal implementation of new DC known
118		Rack and wiring procured and delivered
119		Racks freed (disconnected devices removed, cabled out)
120		Rack placement
121		Cabling between racks established and tested

New DC Layout

Moving forward with the Data Center relocation, we are now entering the next crucial phase. Before we proceed, let's review the completed tasks:

1. New DC selected - A suitable data center facility has been chosen for the relocation.
2. New DC environment Layout prep - Preparations for the data center environment, including grid and electricity requirements, have been completed.
3. Exact internal implementation of new DC known - The specific internal setup and configuration of the new data center have been determined.
4. Rack and wiring procured and delivered - The necessary racks and cables have been procured and delivered to the new data center.
5. Racks freed - Decommissioned devices have been disconnected and removed from the racks.

With these tasks successfully accomplished, we can now focus on the remaining tasks:

Rack placement - The racks need to be strategically positioned and installed within the new data center. This involves considering factors such as proper spacing, accessibility, and optimal airflow management.

Cabling between racks established and tested - Once the racks are in place, it is essential to establish the necessary cabling connections between them. This includes network cables, power cables, and any other required connections. After the cabling is installed, thorough testing should be conducted to ensure proper connectivity and functionality.

4.1.10 New DC Data Lines

ALL	INFO	TASK NAME
1		Project Start
2		⊞ DC Consolidation and Relocation
77		⊞ Procurement
114		⊞ New DC Layout
122		⊟ New DC Data Lines
123		New data lines ordered
124		Establishing data lines
125		Providing tools for data line testing
126		Testing data lines

New DC Data Lines

Upon completion of the ordering process for the new data lines, we now enter the installation phase. During this phase, we can collaborate with the third-party provider to conduct thorough testing of the newly established data lines. The testing can be performed using either a router or your own laptop.

In the case of internet service providers, they typically allocate a small range of public IP addresses, such as /29 or /30. These IP addresses can be utilized to configure your laptop, allowing you to establish connectivity and test the functionality of the data lines. By assigning your laptop a public IP from the provided range, you should be able to successfully ping the IP address and assess its responsiveness.

Additionally, it is essential to utilize this opportunity to test the bandwidth capacity of the data lines. By conducting bandwidth tests, you can determine the speed and performance of the connection. This testing process allows you to verify the quality and reliability of the newly installed data lines.

It is worth noting that there is no need to purchase a dedicated router or switch for this testing phase. In many cases, your own laptop can suffice for conducting these tests, provided it is appropriately configured.

Furthermore, it's important to note that you shouldn't be afraid to modify the routing of your public IP addresses if needed. The process of changing the route typically takes a mere 30 seconds to complete, and the same applies to rolling back any changes if required.

4.1.11 Current DC Test

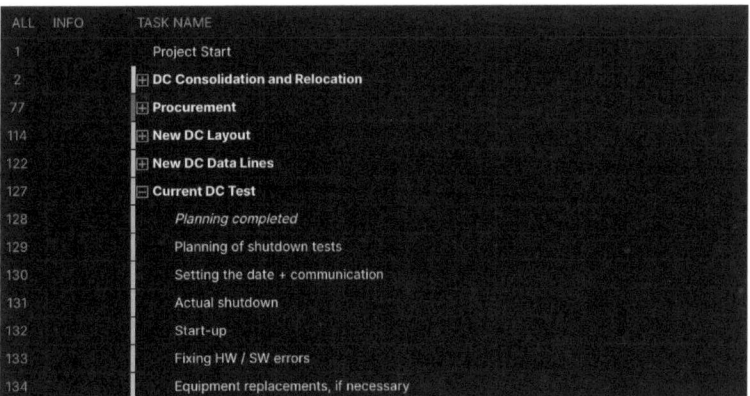

Current DC Test

Completion of the relocation plan marks an important milestone in the process. All the necessary details regarding the devices to be lifted and shifted, the designated racks, and the network infrastructure, including the x86 systems, have been determined. The next crucial step is to conduct a comprehensive test, specifically focusing on a complete site shutdown.

In the event that there are two data centers available, a primary and a secondary, it is possible that the relocation will involve the primary site. In such cases, the secondary site will assume the role of the primary site. However, if the relocation pertains to the secondary site, a total site shutdown is still required. But why is this necessary?

First and foremost, performing a complete site shutdown allows for a realistic simulation of the move day. By ensuring that everything is properly shut down, this test serves as a valuable opportunity to assess and verify the functionality of the systems, applications, and services that will operate solely within one data center. It provides an opportunity to proactively identify any issues or challenges that may arise when operating with only a single data center.

To initiate the shutdown process, it is essential to have a well-defined plan in place, especially if one has not been established already. The shutdown process primarily revolves around determining the sequence in which various components and systems will be shut down. This includes following specific steps and guidelines to ensure a smooth and orderly shutdown, minimizing any potential disruptions or risks.

By meticulously planning and executing the shutdown process, organizations can mitigate potential complications and verify that all necessary systems can be gracefully shut down and restarted when needed. This preparatory step serves to optimize the relocation process, enhance operational readiness, and minimize any potential impact on critical operations.

Objective and Scope The purpose of this procedure is to demonstrate and verify the restart capability of the IT Infrastructure, as well as its functionality after the restart. During testing, any configuration deficiencies, such as manually entered commands that are not part of the final configuration, would be identified if present. Therefore, during the restart operation, only the commands specifically intended for the restart should be executed, and the corresponding operations should be performed. This document does not aim to provide a detailed description of the command-level shutdown of servers, but rather to describe the method and outline the testing procedures, as they can be found in the testing procedures specific to each system.

Description of Testing Procedures The testing encompasses the following main procedures:

1. Verification of system functionality
2. Shutdown of the Selected Data Center
3. Checking the failover process and results
4. Verification of system functionality
5. Startup of the selected Data Center
6. Verification of system functionality

The first step is to verify the functionality of the systems. This involves checking if all the systems are functioning as expected before proceeding with the shutdown process.

Next, the systems will be shut down in a planned sequence. This sequence ensures that all necessary components are properly stopped and any required procedures are followed.

Next, It ensures that the failover mechanisms are functioning as intended and that the systems can successfully transition from the primary data center to the secondary data center or alternate infrastructure.

Next, verify the functionality of the systems. This involves checking if all the systems are functioning as expected before proceeding with the failover process.

After the shutdown and failover is complete, the systems will be started up again following the proper procedures. This includes executing the necessary commands and performing any required operations to bring the systems back online.

Finally, the functionality of the systems will be verified once again. This step ensures that the systems have successfully restarted and are operating as expected after the shutdown and startup procedures.

By proactively setting up the secondary site and establishing its readiness, you can avoid the pressure of performing a site failover on the move day. This allows for a smoother transition and minimizes the risk of disruptions or downtime, hence if you changed the primary and secondary role do not change it back.

In certain cases, it is possible that certain devices may no longer function properly after the shutdown and startup process, and it is important to address and resolve these issues prior to the relocation to ensure a smooth transition.

4.1.12 Reserver time for 15 days

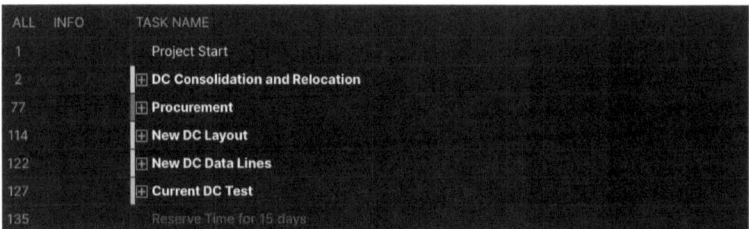

Reserve Time

Allocate a dedicated time period of 15 days for reservation purposes. This time frame ensures sufficient flexibility and allows for any unforeseen circumstances or additional tasks that may arise during the relocation process. It provides a buffer to address any potential delays, perform necessary troubleshooting, and make any required adjustments before proceeding with the movement. By reserving this extended timeframe, you can ensure a thorough and well-prepared transition to minimize disruptions and maximize the success of the relocation.

4.1.13 Notification of stakeholders

ALL	INFO	TASK NAME
1		Project Start
2		⊞ DC Consolidation and Relocation
77		⊞ Procurement
114		⊞ New DC Layout
122		⊞ New DC Data Lines
127		⊞ Current DC Test
135		Reserve Time for 15 days
136		⊟ Notification of Stakeholders
137		Partners
138		Customers
139		Stake Holders

Nofitication of stakeholders

Once you have determined the relocation date, it is essential to gather the contact information of all relevant stakeholders, including partners and customers. This information will enable you to effectively communicate and notify them about the upcoming relocation. By keeping the stakeholders informed, you can ensure a smooth transition and minimize any potential disruptions to their operations. Promptly sharing the relocation details will allow stakeholders to make any necessary preparations and adjustments, ensuring a seamless experience for everyone involved.

4.2 Confirm Date

ALL	INFO	TASK NAME
1		Project Start
2		⊞ DC Consolidation and Relocation
77		⊞ Procurement
114		⊞ New DC Layout
122		⊞ New DC Data Lines
127		⊞ Current DC Test
135		Reserve Time for 15 days
136		⊞ Notification of Stakeholders
140		⊟ Confirm Date
141		Support Company (External Vendors)
142		Moving company
143		3rd party telco
144		Customers (if necessary)

Confirm Date

We have now entered the "Confirm Date" phase of the relocation process. It is crucial to verify and confirm the date to ensure the availability of all parties involved. Consider the service team responsible for handling special devices, as they may require specific access arrangements. It is also important for the lift and shift company to be punctual and well-prepared on the confirmed date.

Additionally, communication with the 3rd party telco is vital, especially if a failover is part of the relocation plan. Ensuring their timely involvement after the lift and shift process is completed will contribute to a seamless transition.

Furthermore, if you have a large customer base, it is recommended to send notification emails or messages to keep them informed about the relocation. This proactive communication will help manage expectations and mitigate any potential impact on their services.

By confirming the date and effectively communicating with all relevant parties, you can ensure a coordinated and successful relocation process.

4.3 Movement Day

ALL	INFO	TASK NAME
1		Project Start
2		⊞ DC Consolidation and Relocation
77		⊞ Procurement
114		⊞ New DC Layout
122		⊞ New DC Data Lines
127		⊞ Current DC Test
135		Reserve Time for 15 days
136		⊞ Notification of Stakeholders
140		⊞ Confirm Date
145		Movement Day

Movement

Movement Day: The day of the data center relocation has arrived, and you have all the necessary preparations in place. Now, it's time to focus on executing the plan with precision. As a best practice, I recommend printing out the rack cabinet plan and attaching it to each cabinet. This will serve as a visual guide for everyone involved in the process.

Make sure you have all the contact numbers of the key individuals involved and keep them readily accessible. Communication is key during this crucial stage. Kick off the day by gathering all participants for a brief meeting, where you can discuss the major tasks at hand. Remember, as the orchestrator, you should not assign yourself any major tasks. Your role is to oversee the entire process and ensure its smooth execution.

Believe me when I say that you will be approached and needed multiple times throughout the day. You won't have the luxury of time to configure switches or cable the racks yourself. Instead, focus on orchestrating the efforts and coordinating the various teams involved. This is a massive undertaking, and your management of the movement preparation has brought you to this point.

By acting as the orchestrator and keeping a clear focus on the overall process, you can ensure a successful data center relocation. Trust in the preparations you have made and maintain effective communication throughout the day to address any challenges that may arise, and undoubtedly, challenges will arise during the data center relocation.

From my experience, some common issues include missing or insufficient screwdrivers, sheared-off bolts, incorrect sizes of socket wrenches, and encountering immovable rack cabinets. One significant failure I encountered involved a 42U-rack cabinet fully loaded with switches and servers. During the standard lift and shift process, it became apparent that the cabinet was too large to fit through the doorway of the server room.

To address this unexpected hurdle, we had to dismantle the cabinet. Disassembling and reassembling the cabinet consumed a substantial amount of time and resulted in a significant delay in the overall process. This incident highlights the importance of thorough planning and meticulous consideration of the physical constraints and dimensions of the equipment and infrastructure involved.

In preparation for your data center relocation, it is crucial to anticipate potential challenges like these. Ensure that you have a comprehensive inventory of the necessary tools and equipment, including properly sized screwdrivers, wrenches, and other essential tools. Additionally, carefully assess the dimensions and mobility of the rack cabinets to ensure they can be easily maneuvered during the relocation.

4.4 DC Return

ALL	INFO	TASK NAME
1		Project Start
2		⊞ DC Consolidation and Relocation
77		⊞ Procurement
114		⊞ New DC Layout
122		⊞ New DC Data Lines
127		⊞ Current DC Test
135		Reserve Time for 15 days
136		⊞ Notification of Stakeholders
140		⊞ Confirm Date
145		Movement Day
146		⊟ DC Return
147		Tasks, cleaning, cabling, etc.

DC Return

Take a moment to catch your breath and appreciate the successful completion of the data center movement. It's normal to feel tired after such an endeavor, but remember that your work isn't quite finished yet. One of the crucial tasks that follows is the handover of the old data center.

To begin the handover process, it's important to restore the data center room to its original state. This entails a series of steps to ensure a thorough and proper clean-up. Start by turning off all the electricity in the room, if possible, to ensure safety during the cleaning process.

Begin by addressing the remaining rack cabinets. Remove all cabling, both power and data, from the cabinets. Take the time to clean up the patch panels, ensuring they are free from dust and debris. Unplug all the AC cables and carefully disconnect them from power sources. Next, remove everything from the room that is no longer needed or in use.

As you clean and clear out the old data center room, make sure to follow any specific guidelines or protocols provided by the facility management. Dispose of any waste or discarded equipment appropriately, following environmental and safety regulations.

By meticulously restoring the data center room to its original state, you not only fulfill your responsibilities but also leave a clean and organized space for future use. This final step is crucial for the closure of the project.

5 Best Practices

Throughout this extensive project, I have gathered valuable lessons learned and best practices, regardless of the size of the environment. Here are some key takeaways to consider for future data center relocations:

- Utilize a hybrid project management approach, combining waterfall and agile methods. The structured approach of waterfall, combined with the adaptability of agile, allows for efficient problem-solving and flexibility.
- Ensure an ample supply of cables, rack mounting kits, and accessories, especially for network devices. Don't overlook the need for sturdy rack mount trays capable of supporting heavy equipment, ideally rated for at least 20 kg.
- Pay close attention to rack mounting kits and have an abundance of rack screws with matching nuts. Always verify the compatibility of screw and nut sizes with the devices to avoid any fitting issues.
- Equip yourself with the necessary tools such as hammers, screwdrivers, socket wrenches, and other accessories. If socket wrenches are used to secure rack cabinets, verify that you have the correct size for a seamless installation process.
- Have a backup person or team in place. With the potential for increased workload and unexpected circumstances, it's essential to have a backup who can step in if key team members fall ill or are unable to perform their duties. Prioritize self-care and ensure the well-being of the team.
- Foster open communication and address any challenges or obstacles as early as possible during the project. Transparency and early discussions allow for timely resolutions

and adjustments, even if it means rescheduling the movement day.

- Assemble a skilled and experienced team of engineers. The success of the project heavily relies on the expertise of the team members. Select the best engineers available, considering their experience and ability to handle complex tasks. Relying on a team of seasoned professionals ensures a higher chance of success.
- Never trust the numbers provided by the customer blindly.
- Always consider the hardware price, license price, and labor cost in your calculations. These factors play a crucial role in accurately assessing the overall cost of a project.
- Efforts should be made to minimize the number of changes during the project. While implementing new solutions like a new VPN solution may seem appealing, introducing such changes during the relocation process can lead to confusion and difficulties in determining accountability if issues arise.
- It is essential to have a variety of cable lengths, such as 5m, 10m, and 15m RJ45 and FC cables, readily available. The distances between racks can vary significantly, and it is crucial to be prepared for various scenarios. Having cables of different lengths ensures that you can easily establish connections between racks without limitations.
- When procuring new PDUs or utilizing existing ones, it is crucial to involve the new data center providers in the discussion.
- Consider the working environment in your data center layout. Provide a chair for technicians or administrators to perform tasks comfortably. If space allows, include a desk as a central workstation for administrative tasks, equipment configuration, and documentation. Keep a nearby cabinet or storage unit for easy organization and access to spare cables, devices, disks,tapes, and tools.

www.IngramContent.com/pod-product-compliance
Lightning Source LLC
Chambersburg PA
CBHW040321010626
45792CB00024B/2088